Webster's Historical Notes

The Alaska Highway

IN MEMORY of
KEITH SVEAN
JANUARY 27, 1938 ~
MAY 18, 2012

First Edition
March 1999

Second Printing
April 2001

ISBN 0-9684875-0-5

First printing: March 1999
Second printing: April 2001

Written by Murray Lundberg
Cover graphic and map by Dennis Saboe
Cover layout by Steven Lundberg
Photos courtesy of the Yukon Archives

Distributed by:
PR Services Ltd.
7219 - 7th Avenue
Whitehorse, YT
Y1A 1R8
Phone: 867.667.4144
Fax: 867.668.6277
E-mail: prservices@whtvcable.com

Printed in Canada

Contents

Introduction

0

The Road to Adventure - in a world that gets more crowded every year, the Alaska Highway provides an unequaled opportunity to see wilderness on a scale that has to be seen to be believed.

As the main access route to a region that was named after the original inhabitants' descriptive names Alyeska ("The Great Land") and Yukon ("The Great River"), the highway offers a unique, never-to-be-forgotten experience for those who come prepared to look and listen carefully.

Built in 1942 as a military access road, the highway stands as a tribute to the determination and resourcefulness of the tens of thousands of men and women who have worked on it, not only during the construction, but through the constant upgrading of the highway, and the maintenance that has, often against enormous odds, kept it open year-round since it was built.

Called the Alaska Military Highway at first, it then became the Alaska-Canada Highway, which was shortened to Alcan before finally being replaced by Alaska Highway, the name by which it is officially known today. To the people who built it, though, it was simply The Road. For 8 months, the lives of 18,000 men and women were dominated by The Road, and for most, it would remain one of the highlights of their lives.

The difficulties that had to be overcome to construct reliable access to the northern frontier were enormous, and the workers involved have earned international acclaim. In 1996, the Alaska Highway was designated as an **International Historic Civil Engineering Landmark** because of both the engineering involved in its construction, and the significant contribution of the highway to the development of the Yukon and Alaska. Plaques commemorating the designation have been erected at Mile 0 in Dawson Creek, British Columbia, as well as at Whitehorse, Yukon, and Delta Junction and Fairbanks in Alaska.

In this book, we would like to introduce you to some of the history of the Alaska Highway and of the Yukon and Alaska generally, and to some of the notable characters who have added colour to the North.

Because of extensive re-routing and straightening, the length of the highway has been reduced dramatically since it was first pushed through. The original tote road was 1,671 miles (2,673 kilometers) long, and by the time it had been upgraded to an all-weather road a few months later, it was down to 1,520 miles (2,432 km). Of that, 655 miles (1,048 km) were in British Columbia, 567 miles (907 km) in the Yukon, and 298 miles (477 km) in Alaska.

Distances along the highway are marked by mileposts (which are now in kilometers in Canada). To make it easier to follow, we have used distances as marked in The Milepost, the definitive guide to the highway; published annually by Alaska Northwest Books, it provides detailed information on the services and attractions along the Alaska Highway and other northern routes.

Between the rolling farmland at Mile 0 and the barley fields at Mile 1,422, you will pass through a variety of landscapes unmatched by any road in the world. From the bare limestone mountains at Muncho Lake to the turquoise waters of the Yukon River and on to the permafrost bogs near the Yukon-Alaska border, each bend in the road offers new opportunities for adventure.

Most people choose to drive the highway in the summer. This is our only land connection with the Outside, however, so travel is not only possible in the winter, but many northerners feel that it is far better when snow muffles every sound. All of the bugs are gone, vehicles are counted in dozens per day instead of thousands, and life in the lodges and communities along the highway has slowed down to the normal peaceful pace. In between, autumn offers spectacular colours and more wildlife sightings, and spring travelers get to experience the yearly rebirth as nature in all its wondrous forms explodes from the icy grip of winter.

Put your imaginations in gear now, and let's head up the Road to Adventure...

Before the Highway

It is often said that the Alaska Highway was pushed through uninhabited country where the only paths were created by caribou, moose and grizzly. However, for much of its length, the road followed existing trails, and for almost 300 miles, roads of varying standards.

The route of the highway passes through the traditional territories of several Athapaskan-speaking Indian groups. These territories did not have fixed boundaries, and the following list is meant as a general guide, describing the territories in reference to current highway mileposts. Population figures are estimates for the period just before contact with Europeans (ca. 1820-1840):

- Beaver - Mile 0-250 (1,000 people)
- Slavey - Mile 250-300 (1,200 people)
- Kaska - Mile 300-700 (500 people)
- Inland Tlingit - Mile 700-820 (400 people)
- Tagish - Mile 820-880 (200 people)
- Tutchone - Mile 880-1150 (3,000 people)
- Tanana - Mile 1150-1520 (3,500 people)

Few of the people on this list had what Europeans term a "tribal" culture; generally, a few families would be allied because of intermarriages or overlapping hunting areas, and those alliances would be in a constant state of flux. The larger groupings above are somewhat arbitrary designations made by ethnologists, and do not recognize the very fluid nature of these cultures.

The climate faced by all of these peoples consisted of long, bitterly cold winters and short, fairly hot summers. The resources required to stay alive in this region have never been abundant except for short periods of the year, necessitating a semi-nomadic hunter-gatherer lifestyle. There were no large permanent villages such as was seen on the northwest coast among the Haida, Tlingit and other peoples. On average, it required about 70 square miles of territory to support each person. Except during peak fishing periods, camps would seldom exceed 50 people, and 10-30 was the most common size.

Martha Kendi and Mary Hager are wearing the traditional baby-carriers of the interior Athapaskans. This photo was taken by Royal Canadian Mounted Police constable Claude Tidd at Mayo, Yukon, in 1937. (Yukon Archives: Claude B. Tidd collection, #7504)

For the Beaver people, large animals such as moose, bison and caribou were the most important food source; a group of 30 people would require an average of 1 moose (over 400 pounds of meat) per week throughout the year. For the other groups, fish was more important, with huge quantities being dried for winter use.

Hunting and fishing techniques were often very elaborate, designed to expend the least possible energy on the part of the hunter or fisherman. Caribou, for example, were often driven into huge corrals made of brush, where they could be easily killed with spears and arrows. Fish traps set in creeks were able to capture virtually every fish that came up the creek while the trap was closed, and could easily wipe out a creek's run if not monitored carefully. Ceremonies meant to honour the animals and fish about to be taken were an important part of most hunting and fishing trips or seasons.

In the autumn, berry picking was an important activity, with blueberries, soapberries, cranberries and many others providing variety in the people's diets. A large variety of plants, including mushrooms, rose hips, wild rhubarb and birch sap were also collected in the autumn and stored for later use.

Throughout the region, extensive trading networks were established long before the arrival of the first white fur traders in the early 1800s, with the Coastal Tlingits acting as the middlemen for much of the trade. Thousands of miles of well-used trails kept trade goods such as furs, meat and fish oil on the move. Some goods which were not easily obtainable, such as abalone and dentalium shells for decoration, obsidian (volcanic glass) for making weapons, and steel obtained from Russian, British and American coastal traders, were much in demand and commanded high prices.

Competition between groups over hunting, trapping and trading territories, although common, seldom reached the point of violence. More often, marriages between the competing groups would solve the problem, and in the process blur the distinctions between "tribes" and territories even more.

With the arrival of fur traders, the seasonal cycles of the native peoples changed substantially, and trapping and trading trails were extended great distances. Unlike the situation in much of North America, where the use of various types of boats was common, most travel in the North occurred on land.

The entry of whites into the interior of the Yukon and Alaska was a very slow process, occurring over decades, and in widely-scattered pockets. Often, as was the case in 1897-1898 when the Klondike gold stampeders passed through, changes were dramatic but short-lived. Civilization also ebbed and flowed with the seasons, as many people would only come north to work for the short summer season.

Particularly after the Klondike rush, when dogs were used extensively to carry equipment, the use of dogs by native people for packing and pulling sleds became much more common.

Although much less common, horses were also used year-round, occasionally being fitted with snowshoes for winter travel.

A powerful pack dog such as this happy mother was a source of great pride to her owner, and within a few weeks, her puppies would have packs of their own. (Yukon Archives: Ed Karman collection, 92/32 #3)

The greatest changes in transportation that were brought about by the newcomers occurred on the larger rivers, where paddle wheel steamboats became common. Between 1898 and the arrival of the highway, over 270 sternwheelers worked on the Yukon River and its tributaries.

Although there were several thousand miles of roads by the 1930s, they could not always be depended upon to provide reliable access. Most roads had little traffic of any kind, and travelers were often forced to spend time locating the route or breaking trail. River crossings were particularly troublesome, often requiring construction of rafts to cross. Several automobile journeys are known of during which the automobile being used was taken apart, rafted across, and re-assembled on the other side.

Ingenuity was a common attribute of many northern pioneers, and was used in pursuit of entertainment as well as survival. This Harley Davidson motorcycle, converted to a snowmobile, was ridden from Whitehorse to Mayo, in the central Yukon, in March 1925. (Yukon Archives: Bill Hare collection #6731)

On July 6, 1934, one of the most bizarre expeditions to ever head into the northern bush left Edmonton. Led by a French millionaire, Charles Eugene Bedaux, it was conceived for the purpose of exploring the region between Edmonton and Telegraph Creek, on the Stikine River. As well as being a very "civilized" adventure, it was also to provide a test of Citroen's new half-track vehicles.

The party consisted of Bedaux, with his wife and a lady friend, a valet and maid-in-waiting to look after their personal needs, and a vast support company of vehicles, animals and men. The convoy of 2 limousines, 5 Citroen half-tracks, and 130 horses loaded with provisions and gasoline cans naturally aroused substantial comment in Edmonton, virtually none of it complimentary to Bedaux's sanity.

Despite the fact that Bedaux had professed to have a strong interest in scientific exploration, and had hired noted surveyor Frank Swannell to accompany them and draw maps of the route, 100 pounds of Swannell's surveying equipment were among the first items to be discarded when the going got tough. Cases of champagne, exotic foods such as caviar and truffles, and clothing suitable for society balls were, however, indispensable.

The logistical difficulties of moving a large entourage through the northern 'bush' were far beyond what any of Bedaux's experts had expected, however. Swamps, mountains and rivers destroyed the vehicles one by one, and supplying the expedition became impossible.

In late October, with snow falling heavily, the order was given to abandon the project and flee back to civilization with all possible haste. At a cost of over $250,000, Bedaux had provided a great deal of interesting copy for newspapers, as well as some valuable information on the logistical problems of taking a large group into the wilderness with motor vehicles.

Although not well planned, Charles Bedaux's expedition had, as he remarked once back in Edmonton, made a start on a land route to Alaska. Mount Bedaux in northern British Columbia now honours his efforts.

The Highway Route

Ever since 1867, when the United States purchased Alaska from Russia, the federal government had been hearing from groups who wanted better access to the new territory. When gold was discovered in the Klondike in 1896, the lobbying for construction of a trail, wagon road, highway or railway intensified, and was expanded to include the Canadian government.

Without reliable, inexpensive access to southern suppliers and markets, it was argued, development of the territories would never occur.

Many surveys were conducted during the frenzied days of the Klondike rush, and construction actually began on many wagon roads and several railways. Despite the expenditure of enormous amounts of money and energy, however, only the White Pass & Yukon Route railway and the Richardson Highway were successfully completed (see pages 40 and 66).

In 1928, after many years of silence, a highway to Alaska was again being promoted, by both military planners and business people. Following a statement made by Japanese Foreign Minister Tanaka in 1927, American General William "Billy" Mitchell started warning his superiors about Japan's clear intentions to expand its empire, the strategic importance of Alaska for such an expansion, and the need for a road to supply and protect the territory.

Although Mitchell's superiors paid no attention to his pleas, Alaskan businessmen took the opportunity to again lobby for a road, using economic development as the justification. An engineer from Fairbanks, Donald MacDonald, became one of the main spokesmen for the project, and in 1930, both the American and Canadian governments expressed support in principle for the plan. MacDonald was able to enlist enough help to get a rough survey of the entire 450-mile route from Kluane Lake to Fairbanks. On the government side, three representatives from each country were appointed to a special commission with a mandate to study the issue, but due to the Depression, no action was ever taken.

Two years later, a group of Seattle businessmen unsuccessfully attempted to convince the Canadian and American governments that, in exchange for the exclusive right to fuel and accommodation sales along the road, they would be willing to construct a highway to the Yukon and Alaska.

Although another bill proposing construction of the link was placed before the U.S. House Committee on Roads in 1935, no action was taken at that time either. The same year, however, following a study of air mail routes to the Yukon conducted the previous year, an extensive aerial survey was undertaken by a group of Canadians, with the aim of identifying the best possible air routes to Asia. During this investigation, pilots and photographers compiled a comprehensive photographic record of the country, which would be of inestimable value seven years later. One of the routes studied was the Great Circle path from Chicago to China, passing over Winnipeg, Manitoba, Fort Smith, Northwest Territories, and Fairbanks, Alaska. Due to concerns about the extreme difficulty of constructing airfields along that route, however, the group's final recommendation was for a modified Great Circle route from Edmonton to Whitehorse and on to Fairbanks.

Based on those surveys, a weekly air mail route was established between Edmonton and Whitehorse in 1937, and was awarded to United Air Transport, which went on to become part of Canada's largest airline.

In 1938, a five-member Alaskan International Highway Commission was formed by the United States government, and by the end of the year, a Canadian counterpart was in place. Canada conducted more aerial surveys of possible routes that summer, and came back with two route recommendations, both beginning at Prince George, in central British Columbia. Both construction and maintenance costs were calculated, and factors such as snowfall depths, elevations, and access to scenic areas that would promote tourist traffic were all considered to be of prime importance in the final decision of a route. The commission also advised that the possibility of using the highway to link a series of airfields be considered.

Anxious to ensure that the highway would be to the best possible advantage of the residents of British Columbia, the provincial government also undertook its own study of three possible routes, eventually advocating a route from Prince George up the broad Rocky Mountain Trench to Watson Lake. Supporters of the highway, however, were not the only ones with plans for the North. The comprehensive plans for the highway were again shelved, having lost out to those in favour of airfield construction. Not until December 1941 would the highway again receive attention.

When Japan attacked Pearl Harbor on December 7, 1941, the United States was taken completely by surprise. The nation recovered quickly, however, and started making plans to defend the North American mainland from invasion. On June 3, 1942, Japan attacked the edge of the continental U.S., launching a massive force that quickly captured the Aleutian Islands of Attu and Kiska.

To counteract the threat of invasion of the mainland by Japanese forces, construction of the Alaska Highway was approved. The decision to build the highway was made quickly, against great opposition from many groups. Journalist George Murry put it in terms that all could understand: "We will either build a highway up to Alaska or the Japanese will build it down for us."

A route far from the coast, where attack by enemy aircraft would be more likely, was an often-stated reason for choosing Dawson Creek as the starting point, but the advantages of having the Northwest Staging Route airfields operational cannot be overstated.

Optimism about the possibility of completing the highway was far from unanimous. It was widely believed that this "engineering monstrosity" would be impossible to construct at all, and few people familiar with the country believed that it could be done in one season. Without the presence of the airfields, the pessimists may well have been correct.

The Northwest Staging Route

The first flights to Alaska were made in 1920 by an expedition comprised of four De Havilland biplanes belonging to the U.S. Army. Since access to fuel was crucial, the Canadian National Railway was followed west from Prince George, then the shortest possible route was taken to Telegraph Creek and Whitehorse before continuing on to Nome, Alaska. The severe weather common in the coastal passes, though, made this route impractical for any type of scheduled flying.

The first air mail routes to the Yukon began in Edmonton, to take advantage of the drier conditions between that city and Whitehorse. The mail was initially flown using aircraft on floats in the summer, or skis in the winter. The construction of airfields suitable for aircraft on wheels, however, was soon made a high priority by the Canadian government. The aircraft of that period were by no means dependable, and the science of flying through bad weather strictly by reference to instruments was in its infancy, even in settled areas. Thus, a series of airfields, between settlements as well as at them, was important for safe operation of the mail flights, and crucial to future development of the airway for passenger flights to the Yukon and Alaska, and on to Asia.

In the early spring of 1939, with snow still deep in the forests, surveys began to ascertain the best locations for these airfields. Of prime importance in determining the sites were the ability to set up radio ranges for navigation, and to lengthen runways in case of future need. The farsightedness of those considerations would be an important factor when the location of the Alaska Highway was determined. Suitable sites for airfields were located at
• Grande Prairie, Alberta
• Fort St. John, BC
• Beatton River, BC
• Fort Nelson, BC
• Smith River, BC

- Watson Lake, Yukon
- Whitehorse, Yukon
- Snag Creek, Yukon

As relations between Japan and the United States deteriorated through 1940, it was clear that, in the event of conflict, Alaska was in an extremely vulnerable position. In August 1940, a United States-Canada Permanent Joint Board of Defense was formed, and two months later, they recommended that a line of airfields be constructed between Fort St. John and Fairbanks for possible movement of warplanes. This became known as the Northwest Staging Route. As well as the sites already identified by the Canadians, airfields were required at Northway and Tanana in Alaska, and a major expansion of Ladd Field at Fairbanks was begun.

Using the Canadian surveys from 1935 and 1939, construction began in early February 1941. A 120-mile sleigh road from Fort St. John to the Sikanni Chief River was widened and extended to the airport site at Fort Nelson. The trail had been built in 1922 to access the river, along which trade goods were then run to Fort Nelson in scows. The rough trail pushed though by the cats was barely passable by trucks, and a great deal of freight was still run down the river as the traders had done. By April, the Fort Nelson airport was already taking shape.

Access to the site of the Watson Lake field revived a route not used since the Klondike Gold Rush. Materials were barged up the Stikine River to Telegraph Creek, where they were transferred to cat trains for the 250 mile overland journey to Watson Lake. The first part of this route was promoted in 1897-1898 as the "All-Canadian Route" to the Klondike, used by those wishing to avoid threats that the United States would impose Customs charges for allowing Canadian goods to pass through Alaska. Although travel in this region is much easier when the ground is frozen, the late breakup of ice on the Stikine in 1941 meant that the first cats did not reach Watson Lake until July 9.

By the time the United States entered the war in December 1941, the Canadian section of the Northwest Staging Route was complete, with radio ranges operational for poor-weather navigation, and some runway lighting in place for night flights.

It then became known as ALSIB - the Alaska-Siberia Route for Lend-Lease Aircraft. Starting with an A-20 Havoc bomber on September 8, 1942, nearly 8,000 aircraft flew this route from Great Falls, Montana to Novosibirsk in central Russia. From there they were flown to various points on the front.

Keeping the aircraft supplied with fuel was a logistical nightmare. Over the winter of 1941-42, over 1,500,000 gallons of fuel were taken to the Fort Nelson airport over the rough track through the bush.

Accidents were common along ALSIB; the deadly combination of severe weather, inexperienced pilots and stripped-down aircraft made the risk substantial. Scores of wrecks remain along the route, many of which have never been found.

In the late spring of 1942 a new B-24 was forced down on the ice of a remote lake after getting lost and running out of fuel. The crew was rescued, but by the time the salvage crew arrived to retrieve the plane, the ice had melted and the plane had settled into deep water, where it remains to this day. Probably the most famous wrecks are those of three A-26 light bombers which crashed in January 1942, in what became known as "Million Dollar Valley" in the southeastern Yukon.

At Ladd Field at Fairbanks, aircraft were transferred to Russian pilots, who often had only a few days training before the arrival of their assigned planes. Although the number of crashes from that point on climbed substantially, it is to the credit of those Russian pilots that any arrived in Europe to fight the Nazis.

During the highway construction, the airfields were also very important to the dozens of bush pilots working to supply the survey crews pushing further and further into the bush. Many members of those crews credit the bush pilots with their lives, as they would often fly food into the camps in terrible weather conditions. One of the best known and highly respected of those pilots was Les Cook. Among his many accomplishments was the discovery of a low pass between Fort Nelson and Watson Lake that made construction of the highway much easier.

Building "The Road"

0

With the general route of the Alaska Military Highway chosen, the massive mobilization of men and equipment began. From every corner of the United States and Canada, men and machinery started moving towards Edmonton, Dawson Creek or other staging areas.

The first problem facing the army was how to get personnel and supplies into the region. Seven regiments, a total of nearly 400 officers and 11,000 enlisted men, were required, and there were only three access points. These were from the end of the Alberta Northern Railway at Dawson Creek, British Columbia, from Skagway, Alaska via the narrow-gauge White Pass & Yukon Route railway, and from Valdez, Alaska on the Richardson Highway. Three regiments were ordered to Dawson Creek, three more to Skagway, and one to Valdez. Two regiments, the 18th and the 35th, were regular combat units, and arrived in Dawson Creek and Skagway respectively with full battle gear, prepared to resist Japanese invasion forces if the mainland should be attacked.
As well as getting the troops north, planners also had to find efficient ways to get 7,500 civilians and 11,000 pieces of equipment to the work sites.

It was necessary to construct access roads at several points to speed up the supply of materials. From a point on the Richardson Highway 129 miles north of Valdez, a 125-mile road was built to Tok. From the White Pass & Yukon Route rail line at Carcross, a 34-mile road was built to access the Alaska Highway at Jake's Corner (Mile 837). As well, a 250-mile cat trail that had been built from Telegraph Creek to Watson Lake during construction of the Northwest Staging Route airfields, was used for equipment and heavy freight. By far the longest alternate route for shipping equipment was by way of the Mackenzie River.

The first parties to head into the bush were of course the surveyors. The knowledge gained by pilots who had been flying over the route of the highway since 1920 (see Chronology, page 74) was of enormous benefit to the surveyors, but the foot-by-foot assessment still had to be done by ground crews. The survey crews, often led by Indians and white trappers, and accompanied by cartographers, engineers and soil specialists, forced their way on foot, by dog sled, or on horseback. For many weeks it appeared that progress was running in reverse, as every dog musher and horse packer within hundreds of miles was hired to get advance parties into the bush to prepare for the construction crews who were on their way. Their efficiency was proven by the fact that within a few weeks, surveyors assisted by several dog teams were able to locate the first 450 miles of road, and have it flagged and ready for the bulldozers.

On the 9th of March 1942, with the temperature at 30 below zero, soldiers and equipment began to arrive at Dawson Creek. As the local newspaper had warned four days before, the peaceful little town of 300 was soon overwhelmed, as 600 carloads of materials arrived in the next five weeks. Until that dramatic day, not much had changed in Dawson Creek since the first large-scale settlement occurred in 1912, following passage of the Homestead Act that encouraged people to move further into the frontier.

Within days after the arrival of the troops, waves of men and equipment were attacking the forest, leaving in their wake a ragged path of destruction, but one that was passable by heavy vehicles. The procedure was for two men on foot (often a local trapper with a surveyor) to locate the general route. A survey party would be close behind, cutting a line that would allow the party to be supplied by pack trains, and flagging it for the bulldozers. A single bulldozer would then lead the main mechanical charge, a team of six bulldozers, three large ones to mow down the forest, and three to stack the debris off to the side. A wide variety of cats, scrapers, loaders and trucks would then start on the final grading. The heavy work of building wooden culverts and log bridges followed, usually by black troops. When required, they would also be cutting down trees to lay across muddy areas, building a "corduroy" road on which gravel would eventually be dumped.

This teamwork was supposed to be conducted on a descending order of priority, so that no segment of the construction would ever be held up by the crews in front. Soil conditions, mechanical failures, and competition between crews all conspired to break the system, but for the most part it worked very well.

A crew from the 18th Engineers works on a temporary bridge across Cracker Creek, at Mile 987, on June 8, 1942. This was the location of Camp 4-W. (Yukon Archives: Robert Hays collection #5702)

The lack of training slowed the work generally, and was the cause of a much higher than normal amount of damage to equipment. The regimental historian for the 18th Engineers, Fred Rust, recalled that:

> *We were suddenly rich, with a million dollars worth of heavy equipment, brand new. To run it we had grocery clerks, fruit pickers, able seamen and cowpunchers, with a bespectacled school- teacher thrown in for good measure.*

As well as accidental damage to equipment, reports of malicious damage done by both soldiers and civilians were not uncommon.

There was also a general feeling that the supply of equipment was unlimited; as one soldier said after losing his 4-ton truck over a cliff, "Uncle Sam's got lots more trucks where that one came from."

A commonly heard rumour about the road, which for many years was notorious for its bends and twists even when crossing fairly level ground, is that no straight sections of road were to be built, so that Japanese war planes could not use the road as an impromptu airfield. In actuality, the road was built wherever it was easiest, often curving around soft spots or outcroppings of rock that would not be visible until you stepped on the ground. Many locals said that they were sure that the surveyors "didn't know where they were going until they got there," but the speed of construction proved otherwise.

"The good old days" on the Alcan. The dark green tents of the 18th Engineers Service Company camp at Whitehorse are temporarily camouflaged following a storm on May 4, 1942.
(Yukon Archives: Robert Hays collection #5692)

Initial plans called for a rough tote road to be built as rapidly as possible by Army troops, with crews under the Public Roads Administration (PRA) following and upgrading the road. It was soon realized that both the Army and the PRA would have to lower their standards if construction was to be completed in one season. Long stretches of the tote road became impassable during spring breakup, and stories tell of huge Cats being abandoned in bogs, with the road being built over top of them.

In many respects, the Alaska Highway was a learning experience for road builders. When it was first encountered, moss and muskeg were dug out and shoved to the side by the Cats; later, it was discovered that it was much preferable to leave all possible vegetation in place to act as insulation, with gravel being dumped on top.

In many places, including a stretch of nearly 50 miles near the Yukon/Alaska border, it was necessary to lay a corduroy road before gravel could be put down. This entailed cutting thousands of trees and laying them on top of the muskeg, across the path of the road; where the trees were small, as many as five layers were needed to support the road.

The rough road which had been built the previous year to access the Fort Nelson airport was of enormous value, saving weeks of work and also making it easier to supply the forward camps with food and fuel. As rough as it was, that stretch of road even served as an emergency airfield for one airplane, whose incredibly lucky pilot was then able to fuel up from a barrel that had apparently bounced off a truck.

The conditions met by the construction crews varied from expanses of dry, open forest growing on gravelly soil, to seemingly bottomless muskeg that swallowed up huge tractors. West of Whitehorse, the crews were able to build 160 miles of road in only six weeks, working in near-perfect conditions. At the other end of the spectrum, the men west of Fort Nelson faced both endless forests and bottomless muskeg, and progress was barely perceptible for weeks at a time.

The living conditions, in both summer and winter, were often brutal, and it was common to hear soldiers say that if the Japanese invaded and took the country, it would serve them right.

For the soldiers, a situation existed that must surely have caused some degree of resentment. They were told that the Alaska Military Highway was a secret project, and their outgoing mail was even subject to censorship. At the same time, the U.S.

Army was escorting dozens of reporters on tours, and lengthy articles appeared in magazines ranging from *National Geographic* to construction journals such as *The Highway Magazine.*

Each construction camp was assigned a radio car, and many men had their own radios. Although men gathered around to hear the latest news about the situation in the Aleutians and other battlegrounds, the war was very much in the background; the men thought, talked about, and dreamed about The Road.

Supplying fuel and lubricants for the equipment required a never-ending convoy of trucks to be on the move. Tankers were occasionally used, but more often, especially during the early stages of construction when the road was not passable for heavy trucks, fuel was carried in 45-gallon steel barrels. When they were empty, the barrels were simply shoved aside, and the "Alcan" was soon nicknamed the "Oilcan" as a result of the tens of thousands of discarded barrels alongside the road.

On the afternoon of October 20, 1942, the final connection was made 20 miles south of the Yukon-Alaska border. At that point, a north-bound Cat operated by Corporal Refines Sims, Jr. of Philadelphia met a southbound Cat operated by Private Al Jalufka of Kennedy, Texas. It had been seven months and 11 days since the first troops had arrived at Dawson Creek.

The final cost of the highway was calculated by the PRA to be $135,000,000, or $66,160 per mile. To put that in wartime perspective, that was about the same cost as one battleship.

Due to the oft-stated security concerns, North America radio stations did not announce the completion of the highway - the news was promptly presented to the world by Japanese radio!

A month later, the Alaska Highway was officially opened in a ceremony held at Soldier's Summit, a suitably impressive location where the road hugs a steep mountainside overlooking Kluane Lake, at Mile 1061. In a bitterly cold wind blowing off the glaciers of what is now Kluane National Park, dignitaries gave short speeches, and members of a band risked frozen lips to play "God Save the King" and "The Stars and Stripes Forever." A short hike up the mountain from the current highway takes today's energetic traveler to a commemorative marker at the spot.

The opening ceremony, however, did not mark the end of construction. Only the pioneer road was complete; a massive amount of work remained to be done to make it truly a year-round access route to Alaska.

Construction of the Teslin River Bridge, at Mile 808. This is the third longest bridge on the highway, at 1,770 feet. (Yukon Archives: U.S. National Archives collection, 87/28 #4)

Bridges on the Highway

**3
4**

One of the greatest challenges that faced construction crews was the number, size and character of the rivers to be crossed. A total of 233 bridges, ranging from small wooden structures to huge steel suspension bridges, were constructed to cross the rivers, streams, creeks, and gullies.

Between unstable soils, unproven techniques for telling the difference between ice and bedrock when driving pilings, shifting river channels, and the incredible power of ice-filled spring runoff, engineers were kept busy trying to keep the highway open.

Some of the methods that were used to build the bridges seem bizarre; many of the rivers between Haines Junction and Tok are both glacial in origin, and run across permafrost. On such river crossings, conventional pile-driving does not work, as the ice present just below the surface is as hard as bedrock. Holes for the pilings on these crossings had to be driven using steam hoses to melt into the ice. The poles were then greased and wrapped in tarpaper to lessen the chances of the re-forming ice forcing them out of the hole. Finally, water was poured around the poles and allowed to freeze, "cementing" them in place.

Few photos of the highway construction show any of the thousands of labourers who built everything from log culverts to some very impressive wooden bridges with minimal assistance from machinery. When the supply of timber spikes ran out, as it often did, men resorted to hand carving wooden pins to hold the bridges together.

During June and early July 1942, and again in 1943, floods washed out many bridges and culverts. Ice and driftwood combined with the high water to destroy pontoons supporting some crossings, shear off wooden pilings on more substantial bridges, and close most ferry crossings for weeks.

On most crossings, 24-hour guards were posted during the period of high water, so that traffic could be stopped when the bridge was about to go. This was considered to be a particularly nasty duty, requiring standing in exposed areas for hours at a time until a truck with a relief guard came along. To make matters even worse, the men chosen for these duties were generally members of the black regiments, who seldom had any experience with severe cold.

Thousands of tons of dynamite were used in attempts to break up log and ice jams at the bridges, but they often did a great deal of damage to the bridge. Success was only temporary in any case; within a few hours another jam would have formed and the process would be repeated.

While members of Company "F", 341st Engineers, bridge a creek at Mile 104, supply trucks take advantage of low water to cross. Photo by Bob Seaton, July 18, 1942. (Yukon Archives: MacBride Museum collection #3553)

One of the most impressive of the early bridges on the highway, from an engineering standpoint, was the 1,195-foot-long crossing of the Slim's River at modern Mile 1019. To be more accurate, it was more of a causeway, crossing the muddy flood plain of the Slim's River, which for much of the year is only a hundred feet or so wide. The bridge was built using timbers milled on the site, and once it was completed, the often-dangerous ferry crossing of Kluane Lake was no longer necessary. The bridge had a unique feature - it was only 12 feet wide, and at several points along its length, pull-outs were constructed so that vehicles could pass. This structure was replaced in the early 1950s by a more substantial bridge two miles further downstream.

The combination of rushing to push the highway through, and unfamiliarity with northern conditions, led to the most spectacular failure in the highway's history when, on October 16, 1957, the beautiful suspension bridge across the Peace River collapsed.

This bridge had been the star of the highway; it seems that no journalists went by without a photograph of the towers soaring above the turbulent river. This was a particularly difficult crossing, and ferries had been used throughout the main highway construction period. The design and construction of the 2,275-foot structure were under the supervision of Raymond Archibald of the Public Roads Administration, as part of the PRA's up-grading of the pioneer road.

Construction of the bridge was accomplished in an extremely short period. Work began in November 1942, the south pier was completed in the spring of 1943, and, with great fanfare, the magnificent structure was opened on August 30 that year.

It was soon apparent that there were serious problems with the north pier. Pilings had not been driven to bedrock as it was supposed, but had instead hit a thick pan of ice which felt to the piledrivers like bedrock. However, the weight and motion of the bridge gradually wore away the ice, and the north support tower started slowly slipping.

Many attempts were made to rectify the problem, but most engineers agreed that within 5-10 years the bridge would collapse. The only surprise was that it lasted 14 years.

The first gap in the bridge deck was spotted by maintenance crews on the morning of October 16, and the bridge was immediately closed. Ten hours later thousands of tons of steel were reduced to twisted junk stretching across the river.

One of the eternal rumours about the highway is that the bridge had been built with salvaged steel from "Galloping

Gertie," the Tacoma Narrows Bridge that collapsed in November 1940. Like so many of the colourful stories about the highway, however, it is not true; the steel was all new.

A ferry was again put into service to cross the Peace River, and a new bridge was constructed; it opened in January 1960.

Between 1948 and 1964, over 120 wooden bridges were replaced by steel ones, and virtually all of those are still in use today.

Speed was the highest priority during construction, and some crossings ended up with three bridges. The Donjek River, seen here in 1942, was first crossed by a pontoon bridge, then by a substantial wooden structure, which would be later replaced by an impressive 7-span steel bridge. (Yukon Archives: R. A. Cartter collection #1498)

Charlie Lake

51

Working on the Alaska Highway, while certainly not as hazardous as fighting on the front lines, put the men in danger both from the forces of nature, and from the machinery they were operating. While battleground casualties are in many cases known to the smallest detail, no official recognition has ever been given to those who lost their lives on the Alaska Highway project. Charlie Lake was the scene of the worst accident to occur during construction of the highway, and its beautiful shores would be the perfect place for an "Alaska Highway War Memorial" to honour those who died.

In May 1942, members of the 35th Engineers had built a large raft to ferry several tractors and a jeep across the lake to an advance work site. While crossing, a severe storm blew in, and the raft broke apart, tossing 17 men into the near-freezing water. A trapper, Gus Hedlin, had been watching the raft's progress from his cabin window, and risked his own life by taking his small rowboat out into the churning waves, not once, but three times. Despite that, he was only able to save five of the men. The soldiers who were detailed to search for bodies on the lake that night reported the most spectacular display of northern lights they ever saw; the Inuit (Eskimo) people of the Arctic believe that the northern lights are the spirits of their ancestors dancing in the heavens.

Coordination between Cat operators and the men guiding the Adams graders they often pulled was critical. If the grader missed a hand signal from the Cat operator and hit a large rock, the machine could be flipped, and several men were killed in such accidents. Although no deaths were reported, many close calls occurred when hand signals among team members became confused with attempts to slap mosquitoes, black flies and no-see-ums.

Even recreation could be dangerous. Many men are reported to have gone into the bush and froze to death. In some cases, they just disappeared, and no trace of them was ever found. Sometimes they were from the South and completely out of their element, but other men, experienced hunters from northern states, also misjudged the conditions. Falling into creeks or rivers while fishing also claimed several soldiers' lives.

The drivers of military trucks faced enormous challenges for which they had not been trained. It was common for there to be an inch or more of ice on the inside of the cabs, even with the heaters struggling full blast. As many northerners can attest, it takes a high level of coordination to scrape ice from the inside of the windshield while navigating an icy road.

When conditions reached the critical stage, many men either panicked, or had reached the point of hypothermia where reason is lost, and died as a result. In one particularly unnecessary tragedy, three men froze only four miles from the McCrae camp near Whitehorse when their truck's fuel line froze. They had an axe, matches, a tank full of gasoline, and a load of worn-out tires that could have kept them warm for weeks.

Several graves remain along the highway. All known ones were restored in 1991-1992, in preparation for the celebrations of the 50th Anniversary of the completion of the highway.

Forest Fire

Just before you reach the aptly-named community of Fireside, you enter a stark valley through which a huge forest fire raged in 1982. Known as the Eg Fire (it was started by a lightning strike near the Egnell Lakes), it was the second-largest forest fire in British Columbia's history. A total of over 400,000 acres were burned.

Fires in the seemingly endless forests of the North are only fought when they threaten buildings, roads or particularly sensitive natural areas. In the Yukon there are two fire management zones - less than 1/3 of the territory (145,000 square kilometers) is designated as the Fire Action Zone, in which fires are aggressively fought, while the rest of the territory (337,000 square kilometers) is designated the Fire Observation Zone, where fires are merely monitored.

On average, forests in the interior of the Yukon and Alaska are burned every 200 years or so. Few people would say that burned areas are beautiful, but, as odd as it sounds, forest fires have many benefits to the boreal forest system:

• Removal of the trees allows smaller plants to thrive; this in turn allows more animals to use the area for food, which is in short supply in a mature northern forest. The stark appearance of a burned area belies the richness of the life it supports.

• Some tree species such as the black spruce do not reproduce until a fire has passed through; it takes the heat of a fire to open the seed cones.

• The removal of cover from the soil inhibits the formation of permafrost. In many areas, the conditions required to permanently freeze the soil are so delicate that even construction of a house can cause permafrost to form on the north side of the building. By removing the insulating layer of moss and low bushes, fires allow the sun to reach the soil and so prevent the formation of permafrost.

You will be passing through many other old fire zones as you drive up the highway. Two others of particular note are north-west of Whitehorse, and southeast of Tok.

In June 1958, the Royal Canadian Air Force was exploding obsolete bombs in a target range east of Whitehorse, near Lake Laberge. Although they denied responsibility, the fire started at the same time and location. The following day, high winds drove the fire across firebreaks, and you can now see the result along about 50 miles of highway. Over 40 years later, the area is just beginning to recover, and now supports a healthy herd of elk.

On the afternoon of July 1, 1990, a series of lightning strikes started a fire about seven miles southeast of Tok. Aided by strong winds and abnormally high temperatures, it grew rapidly; within seven hours it had consumed 600 acres of forest. It would eventually burn 92,000 acres, and come within a few yards of buildings in Tok, despite the efforts of up to 1,200 firefighters and many aircraft.

The Yukon's fire fighting bill in 1997 (a particularly bad year) was $20,000,000 - that works out to a staggering $625 for each resident of the territory.

Teslin Lake

Located on Nisutlin Bay, the village of Teslin is well-known as the home of one of the Yukon's most famous photographers, and his equally famous car.

George Johnston, a Tlingit Indian, was born in 1894 along the Nakina River, about 200 miles south of Teslin Lake. When he was quite young, his family moved to Jacks' Portage on Teslin Lake, known to the Tlingit as "Tes-Lin-Too" (long narrow water). This was an important spot for the Tlingit for fishing, and as a base for their extensive trading activities with the people of the interior.

The Johnston family, which included seven children, lived a traditional lifestyle, trapping and hunting in a region which had very few white residents. Although Teslin Lake was on the very difficult "All-Canadian Route" to the Klondike gold fields in 1897-1898, the thousands of stampeders had just been passing through, and the country quickly returned to its normal state.

While still in his teens, George Johnston took an active interest in Tlingit culture, and traveled throughout his people's traditional territory. His skill as a hunter and trapper, and in building the items needed in those pursuits, ranging from snares and snowshoes to boats, was widely known.

While respectful of the past, he was also very aware of the advantages to be gained by adopting some of the new technology that was becoming available. A camera was one of his early acquisitions with the cash earned from his trapping; in 1910, he bought a 616 Kodak with slide-out bellows, and it went everywhere with him, protected in a hide case that he built to protect it. Carrying a camera on extended trips in the bush, and the logistical problems of getting film and having it processed, required considerable determination, but George started to build a collection of photographs that is unique in Canada.

Teslin, like many northern communities, began as a trading post. Following the closure of a Hudson's Bay Company post at the south end of the lake, the first one was opened in 1903 by Tom Smith, an independent trader. By 1905, general merchants Taylor & Drury (T&D), who had trading posts at many locations in the Yukon, had opened a post at Teslin, and a year-round community soon developed around the post. The village's permanency is indicated by the fact that a post office was opened in May 1913; about two years later, the Johnston family became Teslin residents.

In 1928, T&D had been granted a Chevrolet dealership, and opened a showroom at their Whitehorse store. When George Johnston arrived in town with his winter fur harvest that year, he decided that the shiny new Chevrolet Model AB Sedan in the showroom was just the thing to spend his money on. It took every cent George earned from his furs to pay the $1,172.50, but he was able to get Charlie Taylor to include driving lessons, and delivery of the car to Teslin. This was the first car that Taylor & Drury had sold, and would remain one of the most memorable sales in the 50 years that they remained dealers.

A half-hour lesson in a meadow where the Whitehorse airport now sits was all it took to convince George that he could handle the Chevrolet. Delivery, however, was more complicated than Taylor had expected. Since there was no road to Teslin, Taylor & Drury's sternwheeler, the Thistle, made regular trips to Teslin to supply their trading post there, and the plan was to deliver the car during one of those trips.

The car, though, was much too large to fit on the open deck of the 102-foot-long boat. After much measuring and discussion, a large hole was finally cut in the side of the main deckhouse. The air had to be let out of the car's tires to get it under the steam pipes, and the rear of the car still hung out over the side a couple of feet.

Because of the typical low water level in early summer on Teslin Lake, the only place where the unwieldy cargo could be put ashore was a couple of miles from the village. Undaunted as usual, George enlisted a crew to build a trail through the bush to the village. Charlie Taylor had come along on this trip, and took many of George's neighbours for short spins in the car, until he found out that George was charging them a dollar each!

A few weeks after delivering George's car, the Thistle broke in half during a violent storm on Lake Laberge; all the crew members were saved, but the Thistle and much of her cargo remains on the bottom of the frigid lake to this day.

The Chevrolet, of course, was an immediate hit in Teslin, and on special occasions, George would run a taxi service around the village and into the bush on some of the wider trails. In later years the chauffeur's cap that he started wearing became his trademark.

Nobody but George ever drove the car, and he even gave it a Tlingit name, *Seegwit*, which means "like my son.

On display at the George Johnston Museum, Teslin.

Occasionally, George's timing was off while out hunting with the car on the lake ice. This photo shows the car being returned to Teslin on a raft, after George was forced to abandon it on a distant shore when the ice started to break up faster than expected while he was out hunting wolves. (Author's collection)

Although the taxi service brought in a few dollars, the car's main purpose was for hunting and hauling freight on the frozen surface of the lakes and rivers. A hunting camp was established about 20 miles down the lake, and supplies for "Johnston Town" were loaded on sleds that were dragged down with the car.

One of George's favourite sports was hunting wolves on the lake ice. To camouflage the car for more effective hunting, George painted the car white. For any wolf encountered far from the safety of the trees on shore, of course, outrunning the car was impossible, camouflaged or not, and these hunts were very successful.

George also opened a general store in Teslin, first in his house, and later in a new building in the village. When traffic on the Alaska Highway started to build in the mid-1950s, he moved to a new location beside the highway. George's operation was erratic; prices were set at whatever he thought the customer could pay, he opened the store whenever he had nothing more important to do, and the store was closed for weeks during trapping season. Competition from other merchants caused him to close the store in 1970, and two years later, George Johnson died, at the age of 78.

In 1975, the George Johnston Museum was opened in Teslin. Among the displays of spear points, beadwork and mining equipment, George's 1928 Chevrolet, now fully restored, sits in front of a photo-mural created from his photos. Taylor & Drury had bought the car back from George in 1962; still in excellent running condition, it was used for advertising, appearing in most parades in Whitehorse.

The name George Johnston became known nationally when, in 1996, Canada's National Film Board released a movie about his life, particularly his photography. Picturing a People uses George's photographs of the rapidly-changing world around him extensively.

George quit using his camera in about 1942, although it is not clear why. Some people think that his eyesight was failing, others that he was depressed by the changes that he saw occurring. The bulk of the photographs in his collection show the Tlingit people in one of the high periods in their history, when they were able to take full advantage of both the Yukon's riches and the white man's new technology.

The Canol Project

At Mile 808 (Km 1345), a gravel road heads north from the Alaska Highway. Originally 513 miles long, this road was part of the Canol Project, and ran alongside a pipeline that brought oil from the Mackenzie River to Whitehorse and Fairbanks.

In the latter half of the 1930s, Alaska and the Yukon were truly one of the civilized world's backwaters.

Although the mining output from the region was quite significant, there was still an enormous amount of empty, inaccessible country, and transportation facilities were minimal. Supplying petroleum fuels to the region was not a huge concern, as there were relatively few gasoline engines.

To build the Alaska Highway, thousands of pieces of equipment would be needed, and a steady supply of fuel was essential. Tanker traffic from California was subject to attack by enemy forces, and a new supply was needed for both the highway construction and for the airfields along the Northwest Staging Route.

At the time, the safest potential oil supply appeared to be at Norman Wells, on the Mackenzie River. Oil had been reported at this spot as early as 1789, but the oil seeps were not staked until 1915. Five years later, the first drilling was undertaken, and in August 1920, oil was struck. A small refinery was built, and by 1939 an 840-barrel-per-day refinery was producing enough oil for local needs. It was therefore decided to expand the Norman Wells field, and build a pipeline from there to a new refinery to be built at Whitehorse. This pipeline would be 600 miles long, passing through a virtually unknown land containing everything from swampy valleys to high mountains and raging rivers. From Whitehorse, a smaller pipeline would be built alongside the new highway, to Ladd Field, the Army Air Corps base at Fairbanks.

On paper in Washington, the project, certainly one of the most massive ever attempted, appeared relatively straight-forward. In the summer of 1942, U.S. engineering troops and pipe were dispatched to the end of rails in Alberta, 285 miles north of Edmonton; from there, they were barged almost 1,100 miles to the bank of the Mackenzie River opposite the Norman Wells refinery. At that point, a new camp - Camp Canol (for "Canadian Oil"), would be set up to house the thousands of workers who would be needed.

At the main hiring office in Edmonton, the following poster warned of the conditions to be expected on the job:

June 15 42

THIS IS NO PICNIC

Working and living conditions on this job are as difficult as those encountered on any construction job ever done in the United States or foreign territory. Men hired for this job will be required to work and live under the most extreme conditions imaginable. Temperature will range from 90 degrees above zero to 70 degrees below zero. Men will have to fight swamps, rivers, ice and cold. Mosquitos, flies and gnats will not only be annoying but will cause bodily harm. If you are not prepared to work under these and similar conditions

Do Not Apply
Bechtel-Price-Callahan

In the spring of 1943, the first women arrived at Camp Canol, and a distinct change in the social nature of the camp occurred - variety shows were held, choral groups started, and a regular newsletter was produced.

Morale on the project hit the highest highs, and the lowest lows, judging by comments of the day. The project was regularly under fire from many directions, for reasons ranging from cost over-runs to a rumoured lack of enough producing wells to ever fill the pipeline. For the black regiments in particular, being assigned to the hardest labour work of the project was compounded by a critical shortage of Arctic-weight clothing, so that they were forced to burn lumber and bridge timbers to keep warm.

Despite all the weather, geographic, logistical and political problems, though, the pipeline did reach the new Whitehorse refinery - the final weld was laid on February 16, 1944. With more pipeline having been built to Fairbanks, Watson Lake, Skagway and Haines, 25,000 men (and about 150 women) had built 1,800 miles of pipeline and 2,000 miles of road in only 20 months. It was a short-lived success, however; on April 1, 1945, the Whitehorse refinery was shut down.

Due to the inaccessible locations of some of the camps, a complete clean-up of the project sites has never been attempted, despite much attention to the problem. Now-antique pieces of equipment such as Studebaker 6X6 trucks continue to fascinate adventurous photographers to this day.

Today, the Canol Road is passable for smaller vehicles from the Alaska Highway to the Yukon/Northwest Territories border. From there, it is designated the Canol Heritage Trail, one of the outstanding long-distance wilderness hikes in North America.

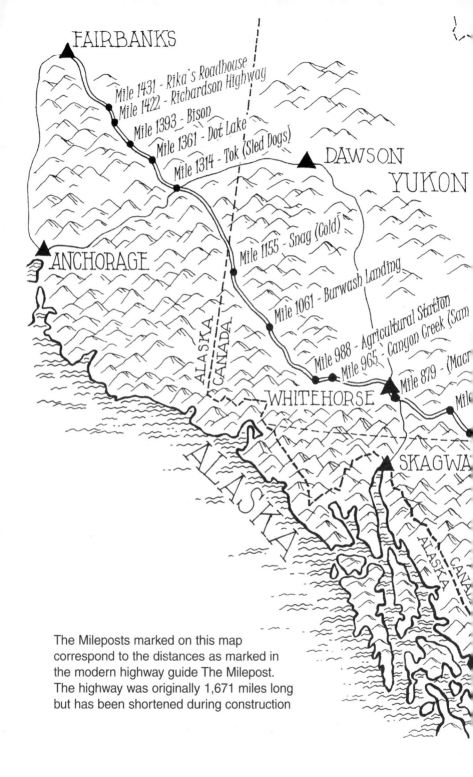

FAIRBANKS

Mile 1431 - Rika's Roadhouse
Mile 1422 - Richardson Highway
Mile 1393 - Bison
Mile 1361 - Dot Lake
Mile 1314 - Tok (Sled Dogs)

DAWSON

YUKON

ANCHORAGE

Mile 1155 - Snag (Cold)

Mile 1061 - Burwash Landing

Mile 988 - Agricultural Station
Mile 965 - Canyon Creek (Sam

ALASKA
CANADA

Mile 879 - (Macr

WHITEHORSE

Mile

SKAGWA

ALASKA

ALASKA
CANA

The Mileposts marked on this map
correspond to the distances as marked in
the modern highway guide The Milepost.
The highway was originally 1,671 miles long
but has been shortened during construction

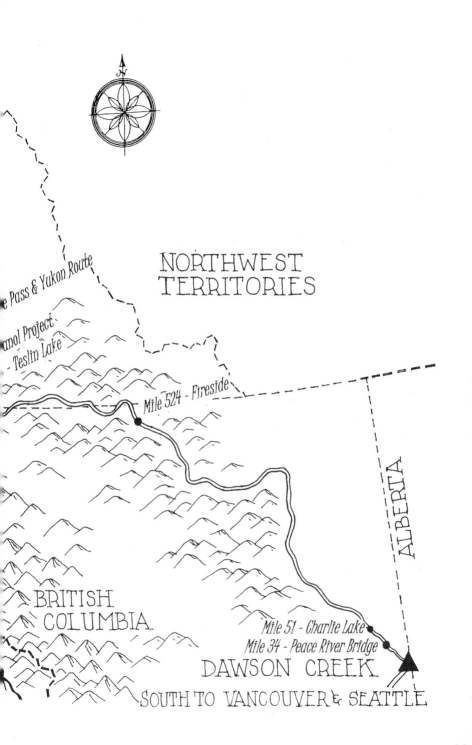

NORTHWEST
TERRITORIES

e Pass & Yukon Route

mol Project
Teslin Lake

Mile 524 - Fireside

ALBERTA

BRITISH
COLUMBIA

Mile 51 - Charlie Lake
Mile 34 - Peace River Bridge

DAWSON CREEK
SOUTH TO VANCOUVER & SEATTLE

39

White Pass & Yukon Route

"Latest News from the Klondike!" trumpeted the Seattle Post-Intelligencer on July 11, 1897. "Gold! Gold! Gold! Gold! - Stocks of Yellow Metal! - Latest from the New Eldorado!" Within hours, the Klondike Gold Rush had begun, and the Yukon and Alaska would be changed forever.

Getting to the goldfields was incredibly difficult. The classic images of the Klondike Gold Rush are those showing hundreds of men struggling up the steep Chilkoot Trail. Photographs, particularly those by E.A. Hegg and Per Larss, captured the essence of that drama, with the images of the final ascent, the Golden Stairs, being the most memorable.

Another pass to the east of the Chilkoot, known as the White Pass, was longer, but offered grades that were not as steep, and was used by thousands of stampeders.

Efforts to improve transportation to the interior ranged from simple to elaborate and often bizarre. Thousands of pack animals, including dogs, horses, mules, oxen, and even Angora goats were used on the trails. So many horses died on the White Pass that it became known as the Dead Horse Trail. More successful enterprises included aerial tramways across the Chilkoot Pass, and the Brackett Wagon Road to the White Pass summit.

The latter part of the 19th Century saw railways expanding rapidly around the world, so it was only natural that railways would be considered for Alaska. Dozens of companies were formed, but few of the people promoting these companies had ever seen the mountains that would face their engineers. Virtually every surveying party reported that it would be impossible to build across the barrier of granite.

In April 1898, however, an unemployed Canadian railway contractor, Michael J. Heney, walked across the White Pass and decided that if he had enough financial backing, he could lay steel across the pass. When he returned to Skagway, a chance meeting with a group who had just given up on their hopes of building a railway would soon dramatically change the nature of the gold rush.

Erastus C. Hawkins, John Hislop and Sir Thomas Tancred represented the Close Brothers and other British investors, but their initial survey of the White Pass convinced them that construction was impossible. When Heney told them that he was sure he could build their railway, they initially scoffed, but after several hours, he had convinced them. A telegram was sent to London, and within days, a complete survey had begun.

The difficulties encountered are the stuff of northern legends. Company photographers recorded blasting crews hanging by ropes over thousand-foot cliffs as they drilled into the mountains, and thousands of men straining to move millions of tons of rock amidst massive snowdrifts and howling winds. But mile by mile, the steel advanced, and locomotives started moving freight for stampeders as each section was opened.

By February 22, 1899, the White Pass summit had been reached, and on July 25 Lake Bennett became the terminus. From that point, steamboat service was available all the way to Dawson City, with a short break at Miles Canyon. To guarantee uninterrupted service, the White Pass & Yukon Route's railway (the WP&YR) had to reach the foot of the White Horse Rapids, below Miles Canyon. The final spike in the 112 miles of rail line joining Skagway and that point was hammered in on July 29, 1900. By that time, a city called Whitehorse was already growing rapidly alongside the new tracks.

By the time the railway was completed, the peak of the gold rush had passed, and the population of the Yukon began to drop dramatically. The White Pass company bought out most of the sternwheelers operating on the upper Yukon River system, and the virtual monopoly held after that time virtually ensured the financial success of the company for a few years. By the 1940s, though, the company's equipment was showing its age, as only necessary maintenance was being performed.

On April 3, 1942, the first troops arrived in Whitehorse on the regular scheduled run of the train. Many of the town's 650 residents had come down to the depot to see if the rumours that had been circulating were true.

When 150 members of Company 'A' of the 18th Combat
Engineers stepped off the train onto the banks of the still-frozen
Yukon River, many people thought that would be the entire
military presence. Nobody there that day could imagine what
was to follow.

*Whitehorse was the only community of any size on the entire
route of the highway. First settled during the Klondike Gold
Rush, it became the Yukon's transportation hub, as freight and
passengers destined for Dawson City transferred from railroad
cars to steamboats.* (Yukon Archives: H. C. Barley collection, #5538)

When the delivery of highway construction equipment to
Skagway became stalled because no ships were available,
General Hoge, Commanding Officer of the Northern Sector, flew
to Seattle and arranged for a whole fleet to be organized exclu-
sively for the Alaska Highway project. Under the direction of
Seattle construction contractor E. W. Elliot, "Elliot's Navy" grew
quickly. Although it consisted of a seemingly haphazard assort-
ment of freighters, tugs, barges, private yachts and a schooner, it
was soon a crucial link in the supply route to the Alaska
Highway, the Northwest Staging Route airfields and the Canol
Project pipeline.

The WP&YR became overwhelmed by the efficiency of Elliot's ships, and Hoge then arranged for the army to lease the railroad and related facilities for the duration of the war. It was placed in the control of a Railway Operating Battalion.

In early October 1942, when a steady supply of materials to highway construction crews was critical, storms crippled the railway's operations. The main bridge across the Skagway River was badly damaged, two smaller ones were completely washed away, a hospital that had just been built in Skagway was destroyed, and only a miracle saved the huge maintenance shops. High in the White Pass, a lengthy section of track was destroyed by a rock slide, and it took three days of blasting to build a new shelf to replace that section of line. Along the first 50 miles of track from Skagway, washouts and slides plagued crews for several days.

Carcross seems to have been one of the best locations to be posted to during the construction period. The weather was milder than further inland, mail service from home was regular, the fishing was great, and there was no muskeg to deal with. The troops even stripped material from some of the abandoned gold rush-era sternwheelers along the shore and built themselves a cabin for gambling and drinking, with a spectacular view over Lake Bennett.

Following the war, operation of the railway reverted to its corporate owners. The development of silver, zinc and lead mines in the Yukon allowed for a major upgrade of the railway in the 1970s, but when the mines closed, so did the railway.

The White Pass & Yukon Route is now just a summer tourist operation. All signs of the line's military contributions have been removed; most buildings were torn down years ago, and the tank farms and pipeline that were built in 1942 were dismantled in 1997-1998.

Ferries were used to cross many rivers until bridges could be built. As long as the truck drivers remembered to set the brakes firmly, the crossings were usually uneventful. Both of these photos show the Takhini River at Mile 915; the 4-ton truck being  *pulled out of the water was full of beer, destined for a July 4th celebration.* (Yukon Archives: R. A. Cartter collection #1544 and Robert Hays collection #5689)

Canyon Creek

965

The pullout at Canyon Creek provides a great location to stop, stretch your legs and have a brief look at several aspects of life before the highway arrived.

The little log bridge across the creek at this point (certainly the most photographed bridge along the highway) was originally built in 1903 on the Kluane Wagon Road, which was constructed to access the goldfields around Kluane Lake. For much of the 136 miles between Whitehorse and Kluane Lake, the Alaska Highway follows the route of that trail

A series of rushes to the Kluane region were among hundreds of stampedes that occurred in the Yukon and Alaska, particularly between 1880 and about 1920. The discovery of gold in what was then known as Rabbit Creek in 1896 sparked the Klondike Gold Rush; although the Klondike was the largest stampede, almost any discovery of gold would cause a stampede to the area. Often thousands of people would rush to creeks that would ultimately yield little or no gold.

The Kluane area was first prospected in 1898 by a group known as the "Mysterious 36" due to the secrecy of their exact mission and destination. Kluane was the focus of several gold rushes in the years that followed, the largest occurring in late 1903.

In July 1903, two of the discoverers of the Klondike gold, Skookum Jim Mason and Tagish Charlie, made another discovery, this time on Ruby Creek, 15 miles east of Kluane Lake.

At the crossing of Canyon Creek there were two roadhouses, one of them run by a man whose name would be immortalized by a Whitehorse bank teller, Robert W. Service:

> *There are strange things done in the midnight sun*
> *By the men who moil for gold;*
> *The Arctic trails have their secret tales*
> *That would make your blood run cold;*
> *The Northern Lights have seen queer sights,*

But the queerest they ever did see
Was that night on the marge of Lake Lebarge
I cremated Sam McGee

The colorful poem goes on to describe Sam's demise during a cold spell that "stabbed like a driven nail." Before he died, he had his partner promise that he would find a way to cremate him, a promise that was carried out in the boiler of a derelict steamboat on "the marge of Lake Lebarge." Vaudeville skits based on the poem can be seen in both Whitehorse and Fairbanks during the summer.

Although the cremation is fictional, the real Sam McGee lived in Whitehorse during the same period as Robert Service, so they undoubtedly knew each other to some degree.

Born in Ontario, William Samuel McGee was typical of many of the adventurous, adaptable people who opened up the North. He was proficient at a great many tasks, and seemed to have an inexhaustible energy supply when working on a project.

Sam arrived in Skagway just after the peak of the Klondike Gold Rush, in the fall of 1898. By that time, the pessimistic rumours coming from Dawson City had been proven to be correct - there was no more ground to stake, nor were there jobs to be had.

Many people, however, were still determined to get to the goldfields to see for themselves, and Sam started hauling their freight across the White Pass. He apparently showed considerable talent as a freighter, and he was soon hired by Captain John Irving to transport all of the materials to build the 113-foot-long sternwheeler *Gleaner*. With some of the pieces of machinery weighing several tons each, that job took all winter; as Sam's crews got the materials to Lake Bennett, they were assembled by other crews, and on May 2, 1899, the *Gleaner* was launched.

As soon as that job was completed, Sam continued on, and worked as a teamster on the tramway around Miles Canyon at Whitehorse for a short period. The flood of stampeders had slowed considerably, but talking with those who continued to pass by him convinced Sam that he had to see Dawson for himself. For nearly two years, he worked for wages in various Klondike mines. Then, having made his 'stake,' he returned to Ontario and married 22-year-old Ruth Warnes.

Immediately after the wedding, Sam returned to the Yukon with his new bride, settling into a small log cabin in the north end of the rapidly-growing town of Whitehorse. With the completion of the White Pass & Yukon Route railway in 1900, Whitehorse had become a major transportation hub, as freight was transferred from railway to steamboats for the trip downriver, and work for men of Sam's experience was easy to find.

It was during this period that Robert Service, then working at the Canadian Bank of Commerce in Whitehorse, became acquainted with the man whose name he would borrow for one of his most famous characters. One of Sam's freight routes was across the ice of Lake Laberge.

Poet Robert W. Service, seen at his cabin in Dawson City in 1909
(Yukon Archives: Gillis collection, #4533)

When the Kluane gold rush started in 1903, Sam and his partner Gilbert Skelly were among the first freighters on the Kluane Trail, and a few months later, they set up a tent at the northeast corner of the crossing at Canyon Creek. They opened for business as the Cañon Roadhouse, and it was soon leased out to Edwin and Bessie Gideon so that Sam and Gilbert could concentrate on their main business.

The Kluane rush was soon over, and most people moved on. In 1905, the discovery of what was reported to be a mountain of silver 50 miles south of Whitehorse caused another rush. Instead of getting involved as a freighter again, Sam used some political influence to get hired as foreman of a government project to build roads to the new mines. This apparently gave him ample free time, as he was also staking claims on the mountain, as well as being an active partner in a sawmill and lumber yard.

The Windy Arm stampede, as usual, did not last long, and the Yukon continued its rapid economic decline. Although Sam was able to pick up some good contracts, he was not optimistic. In May 1909, he and his family left the Yukon forever. They moved around from Saskatchewan to British Columbia, to Alberta, then to Montana, the home state of a large number of Yukoners.

In 1938, Sam, Ruth and their five children were living at Great Falls, Montana; Sam was building highways for a Great Falls company, and got involved in at least one mining company. Ever since *The Cremation of Sam McGee* was published in 1907, Sam claimed to have been thoroughly embarrassed by the fame. In 1938, however, Sam was on the "We The People" radio show in New York to prove that he hadn't really been cremated.

Sam turned out to be a perfect character for Robert Service to feature. He never lost his fascination with the Yukon; he returned for the summer of 1938, and celebrated his 70th birthday while mining on Burwash Creek with Dick Corless.

On September 6, 1940, Sam died at Beiseker, Alberta. He was buried at neighbouring Rosebud on the 11th. Although his name is known because of Robert Service, not his own considerable contributions to Yukon history, the cabin he lived in while he was in Whitehorse was preserved in 1940, and has been moved to the grounds of the city's MacBride Museum.

MacBride Museum, Whitehorse

Agriculture in the North

Three miles past Haines Junction, to your right as you drive north, is a group of small buildings in the middle of a large pasture. Now used by Parks Canada as the administrative offices for Kluane National Park, this was originally the home of the Pine Creek Experimental Farm, where new breeds of grains and vegetables able to thrive in cold soils were developed and tested.

Ever since the Russians' first hard winter at Sitka in 1804-1805, enormous amounts of money and energy have been expended in private and government projects designed to make Alaska, and later the Yukon, self-sufficient in terms of agricultural production.

Around trading posts, missionary stations, roadhouses and other settlements, vegetable gardens were common, although results from them varied widely. One of the notable early successes was that of the Holy Cross Mission on the lower Yukon River; by 1888, they were producing most of their own vegetables, and were even able to sell excess potatoes to prospectors along the river. For most northern pioneers, however, fresh vegetables, fruits and especially milk were luxuries at any time of the year.

To provide insulation, many cabins had several inches of soil on the roof, and gardens planted there provided a small but hearty crop for many people. With the soil warmed by the heat from the cabin, seeds could be started weeks ahead of those on the ground.

The Klondike Gold Rush brought the first large-scale farming to the North. Every possible acre that might produce a crop was planted by hundreds of agricultural entrepreneurs, and it was found that potatoes in particular did very well. Fred Newman cleared 14 acres on an island in the Yukon River, and was able to produce seven tons per acre to supply the booming town of Dawson.

In 1898, Alaska made the first major moves to promote agriculture, when a Homestead Act was proclaimed, and money was allocated for the establishment of a series of agricultural experiment stations. Stations were opened at Sitka and Kenai the first year, then at Rampart, Copper Center and Matanuska over the next 17 years.

Most of the stations were closed during the Depression. There had been some notable successes during their three decades of operation, such as a hybrid strawberry from the Sitka station. There were also disasters which could not have been foreseen, such as the 1912 eruption of the Katmai volcano, which covered the fields at the Kodiak station with well over a foot of ash.

On the Canadian side of the border, the North-West Mounted Police were distributing seeds for farmers to test by 1906. Although many people in Dawson were hoping that flowers would be among the seeds offered, only cereals such as wheat, oats, barley and rye were made available.

By 1908, Paul Rickert had shown the commercial possibilities of small farms in Alaska. That year, from his 100-acre farm at Fairbanks, he produced 2 1/2 tons of greenhouse tomatoes, 15,000 heads of cabbage, 15,000 stalks of celery, as well as potatoes, carrots, peas and many other vegetables.

Some interesting experiments have taken place; in 1917, Joe Knapp had a steam engine set up to warm the water he used on his very productive greenhouse and garden in Whitehorse.

In 1922, the Alaska Agricultural College and School of Mines opened at Fairbanks in response to increasing public pressure to ensure that Alaskans were able to get healthy food at reasonable prices. At that time, only 90 farms, averaging around 15 acres each, were operating near Anchorage and Fairbanks, so of course virtually everything had to be imported.

In 1935, President Franklin D. Roosevelt offered 203 families from the hardest-hit areas of Minnesota, Wisconsin and Michigan the chance to start fresh in a new land, in a fertile Alaskan valley with the melodic name Matanuska. The Matanuska Colony was part of Roosevelt's New Deal, his plan to help Americans recover from the Depression, partly through massive public works projects. A total of 206,000 acres was set aside for the colonists, and although only 20 families were still farm in the valley 30 years later, the project gave Alaska a very high profile, and was the catalyst for many other projects.

Agriculture in the North, particularly when attempted on a large scale, has always been hampered by a combination of short growing seasons, nitrogen-poor soils, and extremely expensive transportation charges for getting supplies and equipment in and produce out. Working to the North's advantage is the Midnight Sun, with the agricultural areas around Whitehorse and Fairbanks receiving up to 21 hours of sunshine each day.

Some small areas have gained considerable fame for their agricultural products. Today, farmers in the Matanuska Valley are well known for growing huge vegetables, with cabbages over 75 pounds, and a 167-pound (76 kg) pumpkin was displayed at a recent Fall Fair in Whitehorse.

Today, Alaska farms produce only about ten percent of the vegetables and meat consumed in the state, and in the Yukon the number is even less. Constant experimentation has resulted in some important advances in the past 20 years, including:

- growing apples by keeping the trees low to the ground so that the snow cover insulates them;
- planting in the fall, after the first killing frost, so that as soon as the ground warms enough growth begins without the shock of transplanting from a hothouse;
- new varieties of grains and vegetables brought over from Scandinavia and Siberia, as well as grains, corn, strawberries and several vegetables developed here.

Burwash Landing

Burwash Landing, occupying a beautiful spot on the shore of Kluane Lake, is well known as the home of pioneer hunting guides Louis and Eugene Jacquot. The region's wildlife is once again the community's most famous resource, but for different reasons; the village borders one of the world's most important natural areas (Kluane National Park), and hosts one of the finest natural history museums in the North.

Louis Jacquot moved from France to Canada in 1894, apparently to avoid military service. He went to work as a cook, and within a couple of years had convinced his brother that the New World was the place for ambitious young men to make their fortunes.

By 1901, both Louis and "Gene" were living in Dawson, working as cooks and investing their earnings in mining properties. By 1904, though, small miners were being forced out of the Klondike goldfields by huge conglomerates, and the Jacquots sold their claims and went in search of new opportunities.

They were in the Kluane Lake area in the spring of 1904 when gold was discovered on Burwash Creek, which flows into the lake from the south. Seizing the chance, Louis and Gene staked a spot on the lakeshore near the creek's mouth, and set up the region's first trading post.

The gold rush provided a few good years, during which time Louis married a native woman from the Copper River region of Alaska. Gene had an astute business sense, and he invested the earnings from the trading post in more mining claims, a single one of which, in 1909, was earning them $50 each per day (a substantial sum at the time). The 1910 cleanup netted them 220 ounces of gold, the largest single shipment to be taken out of the district.

By the time the gold ran out, the Jacquots were determined to stay, and moved into the new business of guiding big-game hunters. Although some of their first hunters were less than impressed (Thomas Martindale wrote about a 1912 hunt with them in *Hunting in the Upper Yukon*), they learned quickly. They dealt with some of the richest families in the world, and bought new equipment as the need became apparent. By about 1920, their fame had spread around the world, and due to the high level of service on their hunts, many women joined their expeditions.

The arrival of the Alaska Highway signalled the end of the Jacquot's guiding operation. Hunting was common during the construction days, all along the route; although there were regulations, they were largely ignored, as everyone knew that the Canadian government had no way of enforcing them. Most of the military officers who could have enforced the laws chose not to, as hunting was very good for the men's morale, which needed all the help it could get.

The first Greyhound bus arrives at the Jacquot brothers' trading post at Burwash Landing. (Yukon Archives: Al Tomlin collection, 92/30 #2)

When supplies ran short in some of the remote camps, as it often did, the men would live for weeks on caribou, moose, sheep and mountain goat, as well as ducks and fish. However, the wildlife in the North does not recover readily from over-hunting, and in 1950, the Yukon Fish & Game Association, in a report to the federal government supporting the designation of the Alaska Highway as the boundary of the Kluane Park Reserve, stated that:

> *"The construction personnel of the Alaska Highway and Airfields took a tremendous toll from Yukon wild life and Indians brought truckloads of game meat into Whitehorse and to the construction camps until this procedure was made illegal. It is a matter of common knowledge... that there is practically no game in the Ten Mile Strip* [bordering the highway].

In camps all along the highway, men kept bear cubs as pets, and at least one had a pet moose. It is not clear what became of the bears when they grew past the cute stage; many of the men were terrified of bears, and would shoot any bear that came within sight.

Although a 10,000-square mile Park Reserve was created at Kluane Lake in 1942, wildlife protection was virtually impossible. Not until 1972 was the National Park established, to fully protect the region's natural riches. In 1979, UNESCO validated the wisdom of that decision, when Kluane National Park and Alaska's adjoining Wrangell-St. Elias National Park were designated as a World Heritage Site.

To learn more about the wildlife along the highway, there are excellent interpretive centres at Burwash Landing, the Tetlin National Wildlife Refuge at Mile 1229, and at the University of Alaska in Fairbanks.

Kluane Museum, Burwash Landing

Snag

The reminiscences of the people who worked on the highway almost always include one particularly clear memory - that of **The Cold!**

In *Truck Tracks*, a commemorative book presented to Northwest Service Command employees, Captain Richard Neuberger recalled the weather during the winter of 1942:

At Whitehorse temperature dropped to 63° below. It was 55° below at Dawson Creek, and a chilling 69° below at the Donjek River on the Alaska Highway. In my barracks niche, the day we ran out of stove oil, my shaving lotion congealed. The cold clawed at you with steel-like talons.

But throughout, the men and women kept working, and apparently even kept a sense of humour. A mascot was invented by someone whose name has been lost - a mascot that is fondly remembered by all who heard his cry in their dreams. In honour of everyone who worked on the highway, we present for your amusement:

The Kee Bird

You have heard the wail of the siren,
As an ambulance sped down the street,
And mayhap you've heard the lion's deep roar
Down in Africa's grim desert heat.

Or the piercing cry of the tiger
At night as he stalks his prey,
Or the locomotive's high shrill whistle
As it sped through the night on its way.

But these sounds sink to a whisper -
You've heard naught, I assure you,
Till I've told you of the blood-curdling cry of the Kee Bird
In the Arctic's cruel frigid night.

This bird looks just like a buzzard,
It's large, it's hideous, it's bold,
In the night as it circles the North Pole
Crying "Kee, Kee, Keerist but it's cold!"

The Eskimos tucked away in their igloos
Toss fretfully in their sleep,
While the Huskies asleep in a snowbank
Start burrowing way down deep.

For this cry is so awe-inspiring
It freezes the blood I'm told,
As the Kee bird flies in the Arctic,
Crying "Kee, Kee, Keerist but it's cold!"

The Mounties abroad in their dog sleds,
Visiting these wards of the Crown
Often hear this cry and stare skywards
With a fierce and sullen frown.

For odd things happen in the Arctic
And many weird tales they have told,
But their voices drop to a whisper
At the cry "Kee, Kee, Keerist but it's cold!"

And many brave men on this base site -
Strong and bold, from a Northwestern State,
Are taking the first train back to Homeland
To forget this fierce bird's song of hate.

They can 'take it', it seems, in the daytime,
But when the midnight hour is tolled,

They cover their heads in a shameless fright
Crying "Kee, Kee, Keerist but it's cold!"
So back to the States they are going
To sleep in a real bed, as of old,
To slip their strong arms 'round their loved one,
Her fair slender form to enfold.

Then off to sleep in warm comfort
And wifey's soft hand they will hold,
To wake, terrorized by a "Kee Bird" nightmare,
And the cry "Kee, Kee, Keerist but it's cold!"

THE KEE BIRD

Tok - Sled Dog Capital

1314

By the time you reach Mile 1314, it will be obvious that transportation is still one of the greatest challenges in the vastness of the North. In the days before a road system existed, the rivers and lakes provided access to most areas in the summer, and again once they froze. But in the winter, deep snow provided a new challenge for travelers. For both natives and newcomers, dog sleds were generally the transportation method of choice during the long winters.

In the 1890s, it was widely thought that any problem could be solved with the proper application of "science," and traveling in the snow was an early target for inventors. In Alaska, the first experiments with machines able to travel on snow and ice occurred during that period, with varying degrees of success. These machines ranged from sleds with large sawblades that cut into the ice, to propeller-driven sleds, steam tractor-trains and even a bizarre device that pulled itself along with a huge screw that gripped the ground.

In Alaska, and to a lesser degree in the Yukon, the arrival of airplanes in the 1920s was the beginning of the end for commercial dog teams. Contracts to deliver the mail by dog sled provided a stable revenue base for many freight haulers, and when the mail contracts were given to bush pilots who could offer faster and cheaper service, most of the dog mushers were driven out of business.

The use of large tracked vehicles for freight hauling had become fairly common in Alaska and the Yukon by the mid-1930s, but dog sleds were still used a great deal. During the surveys for the Alaska Highway in the winter of 1942, several dog teams were used.

Not until the late 1950s did rapid advances in technology result in the small, light machines that we now know as snowmobiles. Starting in the early 1960s, a cultural revolution took place in the Far North as the dog sled teams which had been the main method of transportation far back into the mists of time were replaced by the new machines. In hundreds of villages in Alaska and the Yukon, the mournful singing of thousands of out-of-work huskies was drowned out by the noise of screaming gasoline engines.

In recent years, fond memories from the past, a desire to get back to basics, a love of northern dogs, or a combination of all three, has prompted a rapidly-growing number of people to return to the use of sled dog teams for recreation or for racing. Dog mushing was adopted as Alaska's State Sport in 1972, when, after it had appeared that the sport may be headed for extinction, a major resurgence was underway.

With that resurgence of interest in mushing, the community of Tok, which has the longest sledding season of any road-accessible community in Alaska, has become the "Sled Dog Capital of Alaska."

A sled team being used on a Royal Canadian Mounted Police patrol meets with an Alexander Eaglerock biplane named the "Northern Light," ca. 1929. Although aircraft largely replaced dog teams on mail routes, it was common to use dog teams to rescue pilots who were forced down in the bush during the winter. (Yukon Archives: William S. Hare collection #6811)

As a sport, sled dog racing has probably occurred for as long as men and dogs have been working together; fast and/or powerful teams have always been a source of great pride in Northern communities.

The first "official" race was the All-Alaska Sweepstakes, held in 1908. It covered a 408-mile route from Nome to Candle and back, and in 1910 John "Iron Man" Johnson and his team made the trip in the astounding time of slightly over 74 hours. The race is credited with being not only the first race run to modern standards, but also the reason for the importation of the first Siberian Huskies to North America.

There are now hundreds of races held each year in Alaska and the Yukon. These range from short sprint runs to the world-famous Iditarod and Yukon Quest marathons. The Iditarod, which began in 1973, covers an 1,149-mile route between Anchorage and Nome, and the 1,000-mile Yukon Quest, promoted as "The Toughest Sled Dog Race in the World" has been run between Fairbanks and Whitehorse since 1984. It takes the efforts of thousands of volunteers to put these races on, and around the world, hundreds of millions of people watch the Iditarod and Yukon Quest on television.

The thrill of riding behind a powerful team of huskies can be experienced in Tok and at dozens of other kennels throughout the North, winter and summer; just contact the tourism offices listed in the Resource section.

Christianity on the Highway

Throughout the Yukon and Alaska, Christian ministers were among the first people to push into new areas, and the same held true when the Alaska Highway was first being pushed through.

From evangelists to itinerant preachers and ordained ministers, many men and women traveled along the pioneer Alaska Highway spreading the word of God.

They usually had to hitch-hike from camp to camp, but William Brown, a Protestant chaplain, had his own pickup truck. At several of the camps he visited, men donated their labour and salvaged materials to build an attractive chapel on the back of the truck.

Even though they had little time to themselves, many men took advantage of the opportunity to refresh their spirits, but these services were not universally supported by camp commanders. Some of them considered such activities to be a waste of time, and made it difficult or impossible to hold services in their camp. More commonly, however, camp commanders would give their staff time off to attend services, allocate space for the gathering, and supply bed and board for the preachers.

Often, music was an important component of the services along the highway; the most popular preachers all played guitar, accordion, saxophone, harmonica or some other instrument. Many camps had formed bands, and the religious services provided welcome opportunities for them to play, as well.

When the main military construction period ended, vast amounts of equipment, materials and buildings became surplus. Local residents, used to saving and reusing everything possible, were appalled when the army was ordered to destroy much of it by either burning or burying it. At every camp and community, a cat-and-mouse game began to see how much material could be saved in between the military police patrols. In some rare instances, community groups were able to get surplus materials donated; at Haines Junction and Beaver Creek, community chapels are located in refurbished quonset huts which were obtained this way. The huts were often called "igloos" during the construction period due to the fact that the uninsulated steel buildings were next to impossible to heat. The chapels are still in use, and make charming additions to the communities.

The community chapel at Dot Lake sits on the peaceful shore of the lake, and is a particularly good example of the way Christianity has spread in the North. Dot Lake had been a highway construction camp, and when Fred Vogel arrived from the States in 1947, he bought several of the buildings and started a lodge for travelers. At that time, the only people living at Dot Lake were trapper Peter Charles and his family. Stanley Buck was foreman of the Alaska Road Commission crews along that stretch of road, and he and his wife Thelma used to hold religious services at Vogel's lodge when they were in the area. As happened at many of the early lodges, a small community built up around it, and in 1949 the present chapel was built to serve them.

Bison in the North

1
3
9
3

When you think of the large mammals that are found in the Yukon and Alaska, is the bison on your list? Probably not - the presence of bison in the North is not widely known, despite the fact that they have been here for most of the last two million years. Steppe Bison arrived in North America from Asia over the Bering land bridge. Slightly larger than modern bison, and with large horns, they were replaced by the modern bison about 4,000-5,000 years ago. Fossil remains show that the modern bison were very successful until about 500 years ago, when a changing climate resulted in their disappearance from the North.

In 1928, a group of Fairbanks citizens, headed by Game Warden Frank Dufresne, was successful in obtaining 23 plains bison from the National Bison Range at Moiese, Montana to start a breeding herd in Alaska. The bison were intended as a hunting resource for the Fairbanks group, and it was decided that an abundance of wild grasses and pea vines, with only a couple of dozen scattered trappers' cabins, made conditions at McCarty (now Big Delta) district ideal for the transplant.

Modern bison, standing up to six feet at the shoulders and weighing up to 2,600 pounds, are extremely hardy animals, able to stand long periods of poor grazing. Wolves are their main predator. They usually travel in small family groups, a bull and a few cows (which also have horns) and their calves. Following a nine-month gestation, the cinnamon-colored calves, weighing 25-40 pounds (11-18 kilos), are dropped in May or June, just in time for the new grasses that are sprouting.

The Delta herd thrived, increasing to about 500 animals by the late 1940s. As the bison population was growing, however, so was the human population; the opening of Fort Greely eventually brought several thousand people to the area that the bison found so appealing. The number of bison dropped for a few years, at least partially as a result of the ever-decreasing grazing left after the construction of runways, highways and homes. Conflicts were becoming severe by the 1950s - one farmer had a 60-acre field of alfalfa destroyed by grazing bison in one night! At Fort Greely, almost half a million dollars was spent to landscape the grounds. The bison, however, were by the grass, and ate or trampled most of it. By 1960, the bison were starving. Many had taken to rooting at the garbage dumps, and were dying from eating plastic or from infections due to cuts from glass and metal.

Although they are generally peaceful animals, for several years in the 1950s, a particularly obnoxious bull named "Old Joe" by Delta Junction area residents, gained quite a reputation for attacking vehicles, crumpling fenders and doors and just generally being a nuisance. In the depth of winter, bison would often lean against trailers and cabins to get some of the building's warmth - the resulting "earthquake" in the night could apparently be quite unnerving.

Through this period, the bison were still protected - the Fish and Game Department generally didn't feel that the herd was strong enough to stand any hunting. The exception occurred in 1950 through 1952, at a time when the herd's population was already dropping rapidly, when 25 hunting permits were issued each year. In 1950, 17 animals were also moved to a new range near Slana, on the Glenn Highway. By the late 1950s and '60s, requests for funding to feed the starving bison were being received and turned down, but the 90,000- acre Delta Junction Bison Range was created in 1979 in response to the problem. The project has been very successful, with the enhancement of grazing areas away from farmers' fields being the primary aim.

In February 1945, the Yukon Fish and Game Association was formed, and they immediately started lobbying the government to improve hunting. In a very short time this group, composed largely of people new to the Yukon, would become the territory's most powerful political lobby group, and among their objectives were the importation of bison, elk and mule deer to areas which would allow easy road access to them. In 1951, five bison and 19 elk were released 50 miles west of Whitehorse; with the assistance of a strong wolf poisoning program in the area, the elk survived, but the bison appear to have all died by 1973.

In 1980, the Yukon government started studying re-introduction of bison to the territory, and in 1986, the first shipment of 34 Wood Bison arrived from Alberta's Elk Island herd, which had originated in Wood Buffalo National Park. This is one of the few pure Wood Bison herds in the world, as most have been allowed to interbreed with Plains Bison. Over the next four years, another 92 bison were released, and the herd has grown to about 160.

Bison from this herd became a fairly serious problem on the Alaska Highway - having a herd of bison suddenly appeared in a dip in the road on a frosty morning is an experience not soon forgotten! A wide variety of solutions was attempted, from trucking them into remote areas to hiring a man to drive along the highway firing off noisemakers to scare them away - all were only temporarily successful. As a result of many complaints, and the deaths of nine bison who were hit by vehicles, the Yukon government moved the 'offending' herd of 33 animals to a private farm in 1993. They are thriving there, and can be seen in the large fields just below the highway.

Lottery draws for bison hunts in both the Yukon and Alaska bring several hundred applications for each animal allowed. The reason is two-fold; first, the meat is delicious (very similar to top-grade beef), and secondly, a bison has a boned-out carcass weight of 250-700 pounds, even more than moose, which run 250-600 pounds. Currently, 40 permits are issued in Alaska in most years for the Delta herd, in an effort to keep the population at about 275-300 animals (from 6,000-11,000 people usually apply for those 40 permits!) The peak year was 1996, when 18,000 hunters applied for the 120 permits issued. In the Yukon, 1997 was the first year for bison hunting, when five permits were issued.

Despite game managers' efforts to keep bison away from highways, the grasses on the highway shoulders are irresistible to bison - for travelers, the best places to see bison now are south of Delta Junction on the Richardson Highway, and 50-100 miles west of Whitehorse on the Alaska Highway.

Richardson Highway

1 4 2 2

For the first 150 years or so after the arrival of the first Europeans in Alaska, the primary transportation routes for the explorers, traders and prospectors were along the waterways. With the vast distances involved, building trails was generally not even considered in most areas. The Klondike Gold Rush, however, changed that in a dramatic way.

With the huge influx of people, finding a way to the goldfields through Alaska would mean more development on the American side of the border. This would provide a revenue source for the federal government, which had still not yet convinced many people that the purchase of Alaska 30 years previously had been a good deal for the United States. Several explorations of the Alaskan interior, notably one by U.S. Army Lieutenant Henry T. Allen in 1885, had produced an enormous amount of new information. In 1898, though, the primary routes to the goldfields were on Canadian soil for much, and in two cases (the Ashcroft and Edmonton "Trails"), all of their length.

In 1898, as the gold rush was at its peak, the U.S. Army sent exploration teams to Alaska to locate a practical "All-American" route. The main corridors under initial consideration were the Susitna and Matanuska Valleys at the head of Cook Inlet, and the Copper River area. Captain William R. Abercrombie was in charge of the Copper River parties, and at the season's end, his suggestion that a trail could be built from Valdez was accepted. Valdez was already a booming town, a base for the prospectors who were heading to the Klondike along a route, discovered in January 1898, that led across the Valdez Glacier. This route, heavily promoted by the Pacific Steam Whaling Company in particular, was an exceptionally difficult and dangerous route, and many deaths resulted.

In the early spring of 1899, work started on what would eventually become the Richardson Highway. Cut as a five-foot-wide pack trail initially, progress was fairly rapid - by the end of the summer, the first 40 miles or so (the most difficult section) had been completed, and 93 miles surveyed and cleared. As well as the regular crews, the government hired destitute prospectors at $50 a month plus board, allowing hundreds to accumulate enough cash to escape the country.

The following year, construction on a military telegraph network began. A crucial part of the network was a line from Fort Liscum, at Valdez, to Fort Egbert, at Eagle. Much of the pack trail was upgraded as part of that work. The trail was further improved in 1902 due to the rush to the new gold strike near what is now Fairbanks, and the current highway follows that route fairly closely. During that rush, the first permanent roadhouses were built along the trail. At least one of them, the Copper Center Lodge is still operating (although in a newer building, constructed in 1932).

Following the formation of the Board of Road Commissioners in 1904, upgrading of the road was fairly steady, against the objections of many who thought that this one 409-mile road received far too high a percentage of the annual appropriations. That fact, however, was justified by the government as a prudent response to the proven mineral riches that were made accessible by the road. Of particular note was the mountain of copper found at Kennicott.

In 1913, the Army sent a truck on a trip from Valdez to Fairbanks and back - it was able to make about 50 miles each day, and the use of trucks and automobiles on the road had became common within a couple of years. By 1919, 90% of the traffic was motorized. To finance the highway maintenance, tolls were instituted for commercial vehicles in 1933 - passenger vehicles, carrying from 5 to 15 passengers, were charged $100-175 per trip, with freight trucks charged by the pound. Despite heavy lobbying for decades, it wasn't until 1957 that the highway was paved.

Throughout most of the road's history, the climb from Valdez to Thompson Pass, and the passage through Keystone Canyon have been the main trouble spots. In only seven miles, the road had to climb 2,500 feet, and even today, it's an awesome grade. The trail through the canyon used to be high above the Lowe River (and can still be walked for much of its length), but now is on the canyon floor. The waterfalls in the canyon continue to attract people, from photographers in the summer to ice-climbers in the winter. There are few signs of the early days along the current highway, but it remains one of the most dramatic routes through Alaska.

Members of the 18th Engineers watch as supply truck drivers attempt to get through a particularly bad section. Photo by Bob Seaton, 1942. (Yukon Archives: MacBride Museum collection #3557)

Rika's Roadhouse

1
4
3
1

A stop at Rika's Roadhouse provides a look at one of the most colourful of the institutions in the history of the Yukon and Alaska, the roadhouse. The centrepiece of the Big Delta State Historical Park, it is located nine miles north of Delta Junction, at the point where the Richardson Highway and the Trans-Alaska Pipeline cross the Tanana River.

Few pioneers' memoirs don't have fond recollections of time spent in various roadhouses; they were a vital aspect of life on the northern frontier. Whether they were acting as restaurant, saloon, hotel, community hall, general store, or just a warm place to escape the frozen wilderness for a few hours, roadhouses were found along virtually every route that people traveled on a regular basis. Despite that, little beyond anecdotal mentions has been written about them.

A precise definition of what is meant by the term "roadhouse" is impossible - they ranged from dugouts and dirty tents to relatively luxurious two-storey complexes, located on boomtown main streets and wilderness riverbanks.

Many roadhouses, such as Rika's, were located at river crossings or other particularly important locations. They were also generally the first business to open in a new mining area, so towns often grew up around those buildings, blurring the definition even more. They might be called either "Roadhouse" or "Hotel", without regard to the type or quality of accommodation provided.

Rooms and meals were offered by barbers, bath-houses, freighters, and just about any other business that might be located along a transportation route, whether it was by land or water. For some, operating a temporary roadhouse could supply the cash needed for a special project, and in some cases seems to have happened without planning - people just started dropping in at someone's cabin and staying overnight.

During the rush from the Klondike to Nome in 1900, many of the wood camps along the Yukon River opened their doors to travelers, although the conditions were sometimes appalling. The

"Muskrat Roadhouse", eight miles upriver from Circle City, Alaska, was a 10 x 10-foot dugout covered with muskrat skins, and served "caribou" stew with strangely small bones in it! The cash derived from these woodcamp-roadhouses would allow at least one of the woodcutters to get to Nome to stake claims.

In March 1906, John A. Clark visited several roadhouses along the Valdez Trail while bicycling to Fairbanks, and recorded his impressions:

> Road houses on that trail that year were much alike. They had been built in a hurry to meet an emergency and were spaced from fifteen to twenty miles apart - too short generally for a one-day journey, yet so far apart that for the ordinary horse-drawn rig it was difficult to make two road houses in a day.
>
> Meals at the Valdez end - that is, for the first hundred miles, were $1.50 and beds $1.50 to $2. 'Beds' is a misnomer, for generally they were only bunks built against the wall, usually in tiers of two or four, depending upon the height of the roof. The bunks were constructed of round spruce poles and the mattresses and springs of the same material. Some of the road house keepers, having evidently been accustomed to luxuries before they came to Alaska, sprinkled a few spruce boughs over the poles, and some of them actually had a few blankets to spread over the boughs. After sleeping on one of them, I concluded that the blankets were for the purpose of concealment.

It appears from studying the ownership records of the roadhouses that running a roadhouse was generally a temporary situation for the owners - most people owned their roadhouse for less than two years, and then moved into other businesses or jobs. There were, of course, exceptions to that. The most famous roadhouse owner is certainly Belinda Mulrooney, who between 1897 and 1900 parlayed a $5,000 shipment of hot-water bottles and fabrics into a Dawson lunch counter, then the Grand Forks Hotel, and finally the Fairview Hotel, the finest in Dawson. "Big Bill" Anderson and his wife Emma owned no fewer than seven roadhouses and hotels in Bennett, the Atlin area, Carcross, Dawson and Wynton between 1899 and 1907.

The roadhouses which were built along the mining stampede routes were generally intended to be transient affairs, operating from tents which could be relocated quickly, or wooden buildings which were hastily erected and then abandoned when the rush had moved on. It was unusual to see any of these businesses for sale - the $80 asked in 1899 for Mr. Burt's "well outfitted" roadhouse on Lake Bennett was basically the value of the lumber.

By the 1920s, roadhouse meals were generally highly regarded. There were, however, exceptions. One stopping-place on the road to the Keno silver mines was described as being run by two men who were

> ...indescribably filthy with long, greasy uncombed hair, unshaven faces, grease-ringed mouths and short, dirty mackinaws. Snow containing sawdust, rabbit turds and occasional urination was melted for water and black moosemeat, coated with dirt and gravel from the floor was cut into a greasy pan without cleaning and served with a cup of muddy coffee.(Aho)

Most roadhouses were individually owned; it was not common for companies to be involved in operating several of them. The White Pass & Yukon Route, however, ran some of the best roadhouses in the North, along the winter road between Whitehorse and Dawson. Some of these establishments were owned outright by the company with hired staff, others were leased to the operators, while others were privately owned, with service contracts with the White Pass.

In the Yukon and Alaska, there were possibly 3,000 businesses which offered meals and/or lodging prior to World War I. One inventory of such businesses in Skagway, Dyea, Atlin and the Yukon lists 1,447 to which a date, and location, name or owner can be matched.

Few of these original roadhouses survive in either the Yukon or Alaska - fire destroyed many, and neglect allowed nature to reclaim the rest. However, thousands of people fondly remember the atmosphere and characters surrounding places like the Miller Roadhouse, which was built near Circle City in 1896. In the Yukon, the government has restored the Carmacks Roadhouse, and stabilized the Montague and Robinson Roadhouses; all three are located along the Klondike Highway. In Alaska, private enterprise has been more productive, with several roadhouses having been rebuilt, either as businesses of various kinds, or as private residences. Original buildings such as Rika's, the Cape Nome Roadhouse, the Gakona Lodge and the Copper Center Lodge now offer people a genuine look back at life in a pioneer roadhouse.

Rika's Roadhouse was built in 1909 by John Hajdukovitch, who sold it to Rika Wallen in 1923. The beautiful building was restored by the State in 1986.

Planning Your Trip

0

As soon as you start telling people that you plan to drive to Alaska, you may get responses ranging from tales of terror to others saying that the Alaska Highway is just another road. Where does the truth lie? Most professional drivers who run the highway on a regular basis will tell you that it lies just about halfway between those two extremes.

Contrary to popular legend, the Alaska Highway is completely paved along its entire length. Due to weather and soil conditions that are very hard on roads, however, there is always construction going on at several points along the highway during the very short construction season.

The key to enjoying your trip is to take your time. When you plan your schedule, allow lots of time to look around; opportunities to see wildlife, take short walks off the highway, or meet the people who choose to live here, may present themselves at any time, and can add immeasurably to your northern experience.

Reading about the country before you leave home, or as you travel up the highway, will allow you to really get the feel of the country instead of just seeing it through a windshield. At the end of this chapter is a Resource List of Visitor Information Centres, recommended books and information sources on the Internet.

The further away from the peak weeks that you travel, the closer to "the real North" you will be able to get. In late July and early August, visitors outnumber locals in some areas, and the short summer can be extremely hectic for many northerners; traveling before the rush occurs will let you meet them before they get "burned out."

Many people are intimidated by the vastness of the North, and instead of looking at its beauty, they imagine its dangers. With proper preparation, however, you will be able to see this vastness, not as a threat, but as the key to discovering "The Magic & Mystery" of the Yukon, and the wonders of "The Last Frontier" in Alaska.

Alaska Highway Chronology

- 1787 - the region's first fur trading post, Rocky Mountain Fort, was built, 6 miles from the present site of Fort St. John.
- 1867, March 30 - the United States buys Alaska from Russia, for $7.2 million. Pressure to provide reliable transporta tion to Alaska soon begins.
- 1896, August 15 - gold is discovered in the Klondike, and strong lobbying begins for construction of a land access route.
- 1896-1897 - Dr. Charles Camsell conducts a survey of the Liard, Frances and Pelly drainages. This exploration was very important to highway surveyors.
- 1920 - US Army flight
- 1920 - exploratory flight through northern British Columbia by R. S. Logan, for the Civil Aviation Branch
- 1922 - a 120-mile trail was cut from Fort St. John to the Sikanni Chief River (now Mile 159). In 1941 this was extended to Fort Nelson.
- 1925 - flight to Upper Liard by Lt-Col. J. Scott Williams
- 1927 - start of Yukon aviation
- 1928 - Peter Cramer flew over present highway, en route from New York to Nome
- 1929 - Paddy Burke flying Atlin-Teslin.
- 1930, 1931 - Wiley Post flew over current highway.
- 1934, July 6 - Charles Bedeuax heads off into the northern bush, attempting to take a caravan of vehicles to the Stikine River - see page 8.
- 1935 - Pacific Airways, service Juneau-Fairbanks
- 1935 - aerial survey of routes to the Yukon for the Canadian Post Office
- 1937 - air mail route established from Edmonton to Whitehorse
- 1938 - the Alaskan International Highway Commission is appointed by the U.S. government, followed shortly after by a Canadian counterpart.
- 1939, spring - survey for construction of airports authorized by Canada

- 1939, summer - airport survey begins; finished Jan. 1940
- 1940 - Pan American Airways begins service from Juneau to Seattle
- 1940, Aug. - formation of Permanent Joint Board on Defence
- 1940, Nov. 13 - construction of a modern airway between Edmonton and Fairbanks is requested by Joint Board on Defence
- 1941, Feb. 9 - first cats pull out of Dawson Creek for airfield construction.
  1941, Sept. 1 - Ft. Nelson airport open. The airway between Edmonton and Whitehorse is officially opened for flight in good weather.
- 1941, Dec. - airway operational with radio ranges from Edmonton to the Alaska border.
- 1942, February 11 - the highway project receives Presidential approval.
- 1942, March 9 - first troops arrive at Dawson Creek, Mile 0 of the Alaska Military Highway. The 35th (Combat), 340th and 95th Regiments were assigned to the southern end of the project, the 18th (Combat) 93rd (Black) and , 341st to the north end (based at Whitehorse), and the 97th (Black) Regiment to Valdez.
- 1942, March 18 - Canada approves US plans to build the highway
- 1942, November 20 - official highway opening ceremony at Soldiers Summit, overlooking Kluane Lake.
- 1946, April 1 - the Canadian section of the highway is transferred to Canada.
- 1948 - the highway is opened to civilian traffic, by special permit only.
- 1949, June - paving of the Alaska Highway begins at Fairbanks.
- 1957, October 16 - the Peace River Bridge collapses.

Resource List

Visitor Information Centres

- Alaska Division of Tourism
  P.O. Box 110801
  Juneau AK 99811-0801

- Northwest Territories Arctic Tourism - call 1-800-661-0788
  toll-free in North America, or write to:
  NWT Arctic Tourism
  Box 610
  Yellowknife, NT   X1A 2N5

- Tourism British Columbia - call 1-800-663-6000 toll-free in
  North America, or write to:
  Tourism British Columbia
  Box 9830, Stn. Prov. Gov't
  Victoria, BC   V8W 9W5

- Tourism Yukon - call 1-800-78-YUKON toll-free in North
  America, or write to:
  Tourism Yukon
  P.O. Box 2703
  Whitehorse, YT   Y1A 2C6

- Travel Alberta - call 1-800-661-8888 toll-free in North
  America, Mon.-Fri., 9:00 a.m. - 4:30 p.m. Mountain Time, or
  write to:
  Travel Alberta
  Box 2500
  Edmonton, AB   T5J 2Z4

Books

This is a selection of the best of dozens of titles available. Some of these books are out of print, but all should be available on Inter-Library Loan from your local library:

- *The Milepost* - this mile-by-mile "bible of North Country travel" is issued annually. Highly recommended. 640 pages (Bothell, WA: Alaska Northwest Books, 2001).
- *Alaska: High Road to Adventure* - an introduction to "The Great Land," with photographs by George F. Mobley. 199 pages (Washington, DC: National Geographic, 1976)
- *The Alaska Highway: An Insider's Guide* - lots of good tips on how to prepare and what to see, from Ron Dalby. 202 pages (Golden, CO: Fulcrum Publishing, 1991).
- *Along the Alaska Highway* - a photojournal by Alissa Crandall and Gloria J. Maschmeyer. 94 pages (Bothell, WA: Alaska Northwest Books, 1991).
- *Crooked Road: The Story of the Alaska Highway* - the history of the highway, by David A. Remley. 320 pages (New York, NY, 1976)
- *Mackenzie Breakup* - a historical novel based on a woman's experiences working on the Canol Project, by Jean Kadmon. 252 pages (Whitehorse, YT: Pathfinder, 1998)
- *North to Alaska* - a history of the highway by noted historian Ken Coates. 304 pages (Toronto, ON: McClelland & Stewart, 1992)
- *Rough Road to the North* - written by Jim Christy back when there was a lot of gravel, it provides a good look at the country. 197 pages (New York: Doubleday, 1980).
- *The Sea-to-Sky Gold Rush Route* - a photographic history of the White Pass & Yukon Route, by Eric L. Johnson. 90 pages (Vancouver, BC: Rusty Spike, 1998)
- *This Was No *@^# Picnic* - personal reminiscences of the highway construction project, by John Schmidt. 355 pages (Hanna, AB: Gorman & Gorman, 1991

Internet Resources

• Alberta Tourism Information - the province's official site:
http://www.gov.ab.ca/edt/tourinfo.htm

• Alcanseek - the Alaska/Canada search engine also has travel forums and articles: http://www.alcanseek.com

• Northwest Territories Explorers' Guide - the territory's official site: http://www.nwttravel.nt.ca

• Tourism Yukon - the territory's official site:
http://www.touryukon.com

• Travel Alaska Online - the state's official site:
http://www.travelalaska.com/

• Travel British Columbia - the province's official site:
http://travel.bc.ca/

• yukonalaska.com - "The Gateway to the North":
http://www.yukonalaska.com/

• yukoninfo.com - "Complete online information":
http://www.yukoninfo.com, including over 500 photos.